Getting Better

Results

from the Meetings You Run

Michael Renton

Research Press
2612 North Mattis Avenue   Champaign, Illinois 61820

Cover design by Bob Reddy

Illustrations by Dick Flood

Format and typography by Four-C Typographers & Designers

Copies of this book may be ordered from the publisher at
the address given on the title page.

ISBN 0-87822-214-6

Library of Congress Catalog Card Number: 80-51792

For Christopher and Justin

Contents

Preface

"Everyone knows that leading meetings is a skill. And you can't develop that skill by reading little well-meaning books, can you? You have to develop it through *experience*, and there are no short cuts. Everyone knows that."

True, and also not true. It is true that there is no substitute for experience in the development of skills, and that this is nowhere more true than in the skill of leading meetings. But it is not true that there are no short cuts. If you hadn't taken advantage of the advice and guidance of many people more experienced than yourself in the past, where would you be today?

This book aims to show you the short cuts you need. It sums up, for your benefit, the experience of a considerable number of experts in discussion leading and group problem solving. And it can help guide your experience in the right ways.

But knowing how to lead a meeting is one thing, and doing the job effectively is another. You can only build up your skill through on-the-job practice. So it is up to you. If you put into practice what you learn from this book, you may just find that—*guided experience is the best teacher.*

Acknowledgments

I owe a debt of gratitude to my colleagues in the world of training and development, Dr. Michael Bebb of New Zealand and Dr. Robert Mager of California.

Mike Bebb contributed many of the ideas that follow and, in fact, led me into the trap of beginning this book in the first place.

Bob Mager has always been an inspiration to me. I know of no other technical writer who can put across his message so effectively and yet be so much fun to read. If you think it's easy to write that way, try it yourself sometime.

Overview

From time to time every manager has to run meetings
— all shapes and sizes of meetings.

Meetings to inform,

Meetings to find out,

Meetings to decide,

Meetings to throw up a smoke screen,

Meetings to clear the air,

and, of course,

Meetings to do all these things.

In every type of meeting a manager needs effective
discussion-leading skills. When the meeting is a
series of reports read out loud by individual members,
followed by a few half-hearted questions, these skills
are not exactly critical to the success of the meeting;
but in most cases, running a meeting isn't that easy.
Sooner or later the manager finds that his meeting
has moved away from the relative safety of communication into the more dangerous area of group problem
solving. Quite often he is faced with running meetings which are only concerned with solving problems.

Because problem-solving discussions are the most
difficult type to lead, we have gone into detail on how
best to lead them. However, before we tackle problem
solving, we will give you some background information on the nature and aims of group discussion.
Then we will explain the four steps in running a
problem-solving group discussion. And finally we will
provide a Self-Test (page 81), which will allow you to
check how much you have learned.

1

At the end of each section you will find a summary of the major points covered. This will be followed by an episode from a continuing case study called **Broken Glass**. Each episode will end with exercises to give you a chance to apply your understanding of the points made so far. There are no perfect answers to these exercises; however, you should compare your written answers to the Model Answers we have provided at the back of the book (pages 73 to 80).You may find this interesting, perhaps revealing.

But what if you're in a real hurry? If you don't have time for all the examples, case studies, exercises, summaries, and tests we have included in this book. Well, to start, you can get a good idea of the total contents of this book by just reading through the summaries. This will take only a few minutes. Hopefully this will interest you enough that you will go on to read the full text. It should take you about an hour.

Your next most time-consuming reading will be the seven episodes of the **Broken Glass** case study. If you've got a deadline to meet, you can skip this material for the time being; but you should come back to it later, when you're under less pressure.

There is one more thing you can do to use this book more efficiently. You can turn to the back of the book and take the Self-Test right now, before you read any further. The results should show you which areas you need to study most, and the page numbers accompanying each question will show you where to turn for the information.

Better Solutions through Group Involvement

As working managers we are faced every day with problems on which we must make decisions. However, our ability as managers is judged not on the quality of the decisions we make, but on the *results* we get in solving these problems.

But don't the results simply depend on the quality of our decisions? That depends on the problem.

Suppose you are faced with an emergency job that must be completed this Sunday. You need three people from your six-person team to do the job. No one wants the overtime. Who should work and who should have Sunday off?

In a problem like this, most managers would try to make the best decision. But what is "best" in this situation?

You might think only in terms of "Which people are capable of producing the best quality job?" Then you would ask yourself, "How am I going to tell the people I have selected that they will have to work on Sunday?"

But wait a minute. Surely you are more likely to get a satisfactory job from three willing (if not so expert) workers than from three very capable workers who might bitterly resent having to give up a planned outing with their families and who might let their resentment affect their work for weeks to come.

In this case, it is obviously more important to find the three workers most likely to do a reasonable, conscientious job this Sunday than to decide who really *should* (if you had your way) be called on to do the job. Some discussion is necessary here because the quality of your decision is *less* important than the commitment of the people who have to carry it out.

Now let's take a different type of problem. Suppose you are faced with deciding which size and make of equipment to buy for your section. In a problem like this, is the commitment of the workers who will operate the equipment a critical factor? Or is the quality of the decision the important thing?

It is unlikely that the personal preferences of the workers will be so strong that they will influence the effectiveness of the equipment you choose. You may therefore decide what will be best for your section without any discussion. The quality of your decision here is clearly *more* important than the commitment of your workers.

From these two examples we can see that the results we get from decisions we make depend on two things:

1. The **quality** of the decision made
2. The **commitment** of those who carry out the decision.

The importance of each of these factors will depend on the nature of the problem, but in all cases both quality and commitment must be considered when making decisions.

Now, how can group discussion help to improve the quality of and commitment to the decisions we make?

A group discussion will help to improve the **quality** of a decision when the manager finds it more helpful to listen to an exchange of ideas, rather than to ask each person individually. Suppose the problem is fairly complex. Would the manager working with each individual in turn be able to achieve the decision quality that could be achieved by a number of different minds working together on the problem? Probably not.

Each person would bring her own specialized background (knowledge, skills, experience) to a discussion, of course. But in the interaction among them, another element would be added — *synergy*. With synergy, you get more than an arithmetical adding of each person's contribution. Individuals build on their colleagues' ideas, developing new and much better quality solutions than could have been contributed by any one individual working on her own.

Group interaction adds synergy

You're not convinced? Well, why not work through the case study **Broken Glass**, which begins at the end of this section. You may find it thought-provoking.

Now let's turn to the other element, **commitment**. A group discussion will help to improve commitment to a decision when those who are expected to carry it out become actively involved in making the decision. If it has been *their* decision, they will make sure that it works in practice.

But allowing individuals to participate in making decisions that concern them does more than this. It develops initiative, responsibility, and team spirit. So here is a way to get better results from our handling of problems and simultaneously develop these valuable qualities in our subordinates.

Group interaction develops commitment

It is important to realize that group involvement in a discussion comes in degrees. For example, a manager with a problem affecting his people could

    1. **Tell** his people his solution to the problem and what their task will be in carrying out

his decision, then ask for questions to clarify what is expected of them;

2. **Sell** his solution to his people to gain their support in carrying out *his* decision;

3. **Consult** with them to gain suggestions which should improve the effectiveness of *his* solution, and the way it is carried out; or

4. **Participate** with them in solving the problem together and in deciding how to carry out *their* solution.

As the degree of active involvement by group members increases in these four approaches, the amount of commitment to the decision increases. So when you are handling problems where commitment is very important (*e.g.*, the Sunday overtime problem), the **Participate** approach is obviously the one to use.

Don't misunderstand. The **Participate** approach is not a disguised form of **Tell**, **Sell**, or even **Consult**. It is a sincere attempt to produce a decision which has both the highest quality and also the strongest commitment from those who will carry it out.

Of course, using the **Participate** approach will not always achieve these two things and it should not be seen as the *ideal* approach.

Why not? Well, there are two factors which could make full participation inappropriate. The first is *conflicting interests* and the second is *urgency*.

If you find yourself with a problem to handle where the members of your team are competing with one another (or with you as the group leader) for a solution that will best favor their own interests, the

Participate approach would rarely be the most effective. For example: "Who gets the new typewriter?" In this situation, the **Consult** approach (or even the **Sell** approach) should resolve the issue satisfactorily and with less chance of actually promoting conflict in your team.

And then there's the time factor. There is no doubt that the **Participate** approach does take much more time than the other alternatives. So if you find yourself with an urgent decision to make, practical issues may dictate the approach to use. When someone shouts "Fire!" the **Sell** (or even **Tell**) approach is certainly going to work best for you. You may have to shout a little louder than you'd like to (to get their commitment!), but in emergencies, there is nothing like a few quick decisions, clearly communicated.

Don't manipulate your group

Whichever approach you decide to follow, do not keep it from your group. For example, do not begin the discussion pretending they are expected to make the decision when in fact you have already decided what will be done. They will soon see through the smoke screen and resent it.

The skilled discussion leader avoids any suggestion of manipulation in the way he handles the group. He tells them at the outset what he expects of them during the discussion, and then sets about helping them to function as effectively as possible.

Summary

The manager faced with a problem can use group discussion to improve

1. The **quality** of the decision
2. The **commitment** of those who carry out the decision.

The importance of each depends on the nature of the problem, but unless the manager considers both these aspects he is unlikely to get satisfactory results from his decisions.

Group discussion will improve the quality of a decision when a complex problem requires consideration of many alternatives. Many more and better choices are made when people bounce ideas off each other. Commitment is increased as well when people participate in group discussion. Having a say in the final decision makes it more likely that they will carry out that decision.

Depending on the type of problem and his skill as a discussion leader, the manager can decide what amount of group involvement will best help him to handle the problem and carry out the decision made.

During the meeting he can

1. **Tell** the group his decision,

2. **Sell** the group his decision,

3. **Consult** with his group to improve his decision and the way it is carried out, or

4. **Participate** with his group in deciding what will be done and how.

Whichever approach he decides to use, the group leader will begin by telling the group members openly what will be expected of them during the discussion.

Cliff Aitken, President of Aitken Glass, was at his wits' end. He prided himself on the way he had built up Aitken Glass from its modest beginnings to its present position as a highly respected manufacturer of quality glassware; but now its reputation was being threatened.

It was just ten months ago that Aitken Glass had launched their Aristocrat line of long-stemmed wine glasses. "Purity, Simplicity, Elegance" ran the advertising copy, and there was little doubt that Aristocrat wine glasses were outstandingly beautiful. Sales were all that Cliff could have expected and more, right from the start.

But then the trouble had started. Breakages were reported from all over the country and returns quickly soared to 16 percent of sales. "That's our profit out the window," Cliff had told Bill Martin, the young Development Director of Aitken Glass. "I want you to get out there and solve the problem . . . fast!"

Bill did a pretty good job. He started in the plant with Quality Control, then Packaging and Shipping, then Marketing. And he really scratched around thoroughly wherever he went. He interviewed dozens of interested people, starting with Aitken employees, then shippers, wholesalers, and retailers, and eventually even talking to some of the dissatisfied customers who had bought and returned broken Aristocrat glasses.

11

On his travels, Bill established several important points:

1. Flaws in the glass were not to blame.

2. Breakages by the end user in the home were rare.

3. Most breakages occurred inside the six-glass cardboard boxes in which the glasses were packed.

4. Although robust, the packaging was unable to protect the fragile stems from breaking when the boxes were mishandled.

"So what do you suggest doing?" Cliff wanted to know at one of their many report-back sessions.

"Well, we could thicken the stems . . . ," Bill began hesitantly. He knew how proud Cliff was of the graceful sweep of elegance that was the distinctive feature of the Aristocrat wine glasses.

Cliff scowled and Bill quickly went on, "Or we could strengthen the boxes, put in extra padding. And put a brighter, more eye-catching 'Glassware' warning on each box."

"Do it," said Cliff.

Three months later, an uncomfortable Bill Martin was back before Cliff Aitken.

"It didn't work, did it?" asked Cliff.

"No," said Bill unhappily.

"What now?"

"Well, I thought we might rework our discount structure. We must give the retail stores an incentive to prevent these breakages. It's too easy for them to claim the breakages are due to the inherent weakness of the thin stems ... or to inadequate protection in our packaging. At present, if their people break the glasses, the total replacement cost is carried by us. Why should they bother to ride their staff for carelessness?"

"OK. Let's try it," said Cliff, a man of few words and quick decisions.

Now it's your turn ...

a) How do you feel about the way Cliff Aitken has tackled this problem so far?

b) Which method (Tell, Sell, Consult, or Participate) or combination of methods is Cliff using?

c) Do you agree or disagree with his approach? Why?

Broken Glass will be continued shortly, but first a little more information about effective discussion leading ...

Elements of Effective Group Discussion

In an effective group discussion the discussion leader guides the group to a better quality solution to a problem they are concerned with and/or greater commitment to a decision they will be carrying out. Such a group discussion differs from social conversation in two main respects.

Objective. It has an objective—a definite aim. This may be to solve a problem, to improve individual performance, to improve team effectiveness or morale, or all of these. The best test of the effectiveness of a group discussion is to ask the question "To what extent did you achieve your objective?"

Discussion leader. It has a discussion leader or chairman to guide the discussion. This guidance is done in terms of the objective of the discussion and the needs of both the individual members of the group and the group as a whole.

There is also another factor involved in effective group discussion.

Friendly team spirit. Group discussion relies for its effectiveness on the involvement of the group members and on the exchange of ideas among the group members. Because of this, the discussion leader needs to establish a friendly team spirit—an atmosphere in which each member feels free to contribute to the discussion with candor and without fear of criticism or retaliation.

An effective discussion leader therefore delays passing judgment on the contributions of members.

15

Instead, by skillful questioning, he helps everyone to understand the different views being presented.

Try to keep a friendly team spirit

For example, he may say to a member who has just complained about the amount of time he has to spend sitting in meetings, "Do you feel that we are spending too much time on *our* meetings?" If the member replies, "Yes, I'm afraid so," the leader might ask, "Why do you say that?" After exploring the member's reasons, the leader might say, "Can you suggest any way in which we could speed our meetings up?"

If group members feel that others are trying to understand their points of view rather than criticize, they are much more likely to listen and to consider the points being made by others. They will try to weigh, as objectively as possible, the ideas and experience of others. They may even begin to reconsider their own viewpoints.

However, if they feel they are being attacked, their emotional defenses will quickly come up and cut off all further exchange of ideas. This may take the form of resentful withdrawal from the discussion, and one member may suddenly become silent. Alternatively, it may provoke a strong counterattack on the person who criticized them, and two adults may begin squabbling like children. Either way, the effectiveness of the discussion will be damaged as soon as the friendly team spirit is replaced by a threatening atmosphere.

Summary

In an effective group discussion you will recognize

1. an **objective**, a definite end result to be achieved

2. a **discussion leader** to help the group reach the objective

3. a **friendly team spirit** which encourages everyone to contribute fully without fear of criticism.

"I've called this meeting," began Cliff Aitken, "because I'm not satisfied with the progress we're making to reduce returns on the Aristocrat line."

He looked around the table. Five of his senior executives noted his grim expression with varying degrees of concern.

"I bet I know exactly what each of you is going to say," thought Cliff. "Bill wants me to give in and thicken the stems. It might solve the breakage problem but it would destroy the design . . . and our reputation."

His glance shifted to Ted Hughes, Vice-President, Marketing. "Ted wants to train the retail store staff to handle and sell our products more effectively. It would cost a fortune and, anyway, I'm not sure it would solve the problem."

He looked at Cas Kolicki, Vice-President, Manufacturing. "Cas wants me to raise the price to cover the cost of the breakages. We may have to do that, but I'm not sure how it would affect sales."

He turned to Frank Tallon, Distribution Manager. "Frank has had to take most of the customer noise on this one. I'm sure he'd like to see us abort the Aristocrat line completely."

He glanced briefly at Jean Hemp, his Financial Controller. "Jean's a sensible person. She'll go along with whatever we decide . . . so long as the numbers come out right, that is."

"May I say something, Mr. Aitken?" broke in Bill.

"Sure."

"Well, I agree that the returns are still running at much too high a level. But we have made some progress."

"Some progress!" cut in Frank. "You should see my desk. Covered with return claims. And my warehouse. Knee deep in broken glass!"

Cliff smiled. Frank was inclined to overdramatize his difficulties.

"OK, Frank," snapped Bill. "I've been living with this nightmare for nine months now, trying to find a solution. I've had my ear bashed by scores of people and we've tried half-a-dozen ideas. None of them has reduced the breakages to acceptable levels. So what's your solution, Bright Eyes?"

"It's not my job to find solutions to your problems," sneered Frank. "Why don't you just admit that the Aristocrat line is not a practical design? Give it up and start over again, Bill."

Let's have your ideas now . . .

a) How effectively is Cliff Aitken leading this discussion?

b) Is the objective clear? Could he have done better?

c) How is Cliff playing his role as discussion leader? Would you have done anything differently?

d) What about the friendly team spirit? Is the exchange between Frank and Bill really hurting the discussion?

We'll be returning to **Broken Glass** after we've had a closer look at the role of the discussion leader . . .

The discussion leader must continually do four things during the group discussion:

1. **Stimulate**
2. **Control**
3. **Support**
4. **Observe.**

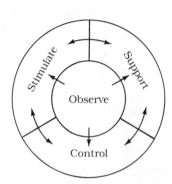

Let's take each in turn.

Stimulate. The discussion leader must stimulate the group members to take part. To begin with, he does this by providing information on the problem or situation being discussed. It is obviously necessary that the discussion leader provide the objective of the discussion and many of the basic facts; he should also point out the value of the objective to each group member.

The effective discussion leader stimulates the members throughout the discussion by continually asking questions and exploring ideas, and by occasionally summarizing the contributions made. He uses expressions like "Let's get this clear. Are you suggesting that . . . ?" "Could you give us an example to help us understand your point?" and "It would be helpful to get the views of a few others on this. How do you feel about Jan's idea, Herb?"

21

Of course, some managers feel they already do a great job of stimulating the group members to participate in their meetings. They sound something like this:

"Well, I think we've spent enough time discussing this problem. It's time we came to a decision on what has to be done. I've given this a lot of thought and I think we should double our output and halve our costs. Are we all in agreement on this? Of course, I want you to realize that this is only a suggestion. But I think you should remember *who* is making the suggestion."

Don't discourage participation by signaling your opinion

A bit exaggerated perhaps, but many managers cut off their source of ideas and enthusiasm the moment they open the discussion with the two dreaded words "I think." After that, any manager is fooling himself if he expects much more in the way of participation from his staff than a verbal round of applause. The effective discussion leader plays down his own ideas *until* he has successfully stimulated the group members to exchange and develop their own thoughts and suggestions.

One important way to do this is to use **open questions**. These are questions that encourage others to contribute their ideas and experience. The best ones begin with these words: How; Which; When; Who; Where; Why; or What. Let's look at a few examples.

"*How* do you feel about that point, Joyce?"

"*Which* of these items would you say is the most important to us?"

"*When* did we last have a customer complaint of this kind?"

"*Who* would be the best person to investigate this method more carefully?"

"*Where* would be the best place to try this out?"

"*Why* are you resisting Jim's suggestion so strongly, Jeff?"

"*What* would you say is the best answer, Bob?"

Closed questions, on the other hand, are not very helpful in getting a person to talk. These are questions that can be answered with a simple yes or no. They may start with: Do you; Will you; or Have you. Here are a few examples.

"*Do you* agree that this is the real problem, George?"

"*Will you* make sure that this project is carried through?"

"*Have you* checked the accuracy of those figures, Joan?"

Closed questions discourage further contributions from group members. However, they *do* have a place in problem-solving discussions.

Suppose the discussion leader is trying to get the group to consider a probable but not-too-popular solution. She can use a closed question, in which the answer is strongly implied, to influence their thinking. For example: "Aren't we going to have to work overtime to meet the deadline on this job?"

This can be a very necessary line to take from time to time, but it shouldn't be overdone. If the leader suddenly catches herself asking too many closed questions (and hence doing most of the talking), she should back off for a minute. She can give herself time to think and restore the balance by throwing in a few open questions, such as "But what's your opinion?" or the old reliable "Why do you say that?"

Control. The leader must control the group members. No one likes to feel that time is going by with no progress being made; yet this is likely to occur if the discussion leader fails to keep the discussion on course.

This does not mean that he must strictly or abruptly control the discussion, which might cause resentment and destroy the friendly team spirit which is so important to success. Instead, he should keep the discussion moving forward by gently redirecting members who have strayed from the point and by periodically summing up the progress that is being made. This acts as a reminder of the direction that the discussion should be going in if the objective is to be reached in the time available; it also helps to prevent members from going over the same old point again in a slightly different way.

For example: "Now let's hold it a moment. We've already decided that the main cause of the trouble, which should be tackled first, is poor verbal communication. Is it worthwhile to spend time on a number of other causes at this point? Perhaps we can come

Redirect straying group members

back to these in a later meeting. Now let's get back to discussing how we are going to improve our verbal communication."

Support. The leader must support every member who wishes to take part. She does this by maintaining the right of each individual to express his own opinion and by continually drawing attention to the value of considering different points of view. For example: "Peter may have a good point here. Let's give him a chance to explain what he has in mind."

The effective discussion leader will also provide support to group members by keeping any disagreement or evaluation centered on the problem rather than the individual. For example, she might say, "That's an unusual idea" rather than "I'm surprised at you putting forward an idea like that."

26

Observe. In order to stimulate, control, and support the group members effectively during the discussion, the discussion leader must continually observe the group. He must be aware of what is going on within the group and within each individual; be sensitive to the group atmosphere; and be able to spot underlying resistance or conflicts which can only be reconciled if they are brought out into the open and discussed. For example, the leader might say, "I get the impression that you're not quite happy about what Carol has suggested, Chuck. Am I right?" Only by skillful observation will the discussion leader know which balance of stimulation, control, or support will best help the group to progress towards the objective.

Keep an eye on your own behavior

Although the effective discussion leader concentrates on the group, he also keeps an eye on his own behavior. He tries to recognize emotional reactions which may be developing in himself, for the moment the discussion leader loses control of his emotions, the friendly team spirit he is trying to maintain is in danger of being destroyed. This is the most difficult aspect of discussion leading. It requires considerable insight and, as with all the other skills of discussion leading, it can only be developed by practice.

Summary

The effective discussion leader

1. **Stimulates** the group members to take part
2. **Controls** the discussion to ensure effective use of the time
3. **Supports** the right of every member to freely state his views on the subject
4. **Observes** what is going on under the surface of the discussion so that he is able to bring out underlying conflicts or resistance in group members.

Cliff Aitken held up his hand. "Can we just hold it there Bill, Frank. I'm not sure this line of discussion will prove all that helpful." Cliff looked around the table."With the help of each one of you, Bill *has* made progress. But we aren't home yet. And we're going to need everyone's ideas and assistance to crack this one. So let's concentrate on pulling together, not apart."

There was a long, uncomfortable silence. Cliff looked at each person in turn and then went on. "Now let's recap on where we stand at present. Bill, will you summarize what we've done so far and what results we've seen?"

Bill cleared his throat. He spoke rapidly and well, tracing the full history of the Aristocrat line. He assessed both its strengths and weaknesses and he did so as objectively as he was able. Occasionally Cliff interrupted him to ask a question or to point out that he was going into unnecessary detail. No one else spoke.

"Thank you, Bill. That's been very helpful." Cliff turned to Jean Hemp. "Jean, will you fill us in on the financial implications of what we have heard?"

"Well, Mr. Aitken, the recent drop in percentage returns has turned the loss on the Aristocrat line to a break-even position. Unless we raise the price, we will need to reduce our returns by a further 8 percent before we can achieve our budgeted profit."

"Why don't we do that?" cut in Cas. "It's a superb glass, but it's very difficult to manufacture in volume.

In my opinion it is being sold at a ridiculously low price."

"That's nonsense!" exploded Ted. "You have no idea of the competition we are facing from Japan. It's a cutthroat business we're in and it's time you realized that, Cas."

"Don't be so defensive, Ted," said Cliff quickly. "I'm sure Cas realizes we're selling in a competitive market, but he may have a point about the price. Ted, what percentage of our current sales do you think we might lose if we raised the price by, say, 10 percent?"

"I'd need to do my homework before answering that, Mr. Aitken," answered Ted lamely.

"How long would it take?"

"About a week, Mr. Aitken."

"OK. Let me have your assessment as soon as it's ready."

"Will do."

"Good. Now, are there any other ideas that anyone would like to put forward at this point?" The question was greeted by five blank expressions.

"All right. That seems to be all we can accomplish today. We'll meet again next Monday at the same time. And, by the way, I'd like all of you to give this problem a lot of thought before then. We really need your ideas.

Now for your comments . . .

a) How do you feel Cliff is filling his role as discussion leader?

b) Is he stimulating the group members to take part? Could he have done this more effectively at any point?

c) What about his control? Is he making the best use of time in the discussion? Why do you say that?

d) Is Cliff giving each person the support he needs to contribute fully to the discussion? Could this have been improved anywhere?

e) How good an observer is Cliff? Have you spotted any underlying conflicts that he seems to have missed?

We'll pick up the story of **Broken Glass** again. But first we need to begin considering the four main steps in leading problem-solving discussions:

1. Prepare for the discussion.

2. Introduce the discussion.

3. Lead the discussion.

4. Conclude the discussion.

Let's start with the all-important subject of preparation . . .

Step 1: Prepare for the Discussion

Identify the real problem. Begin by asking "What exactly has gone wrong (or could go wrong) with what?" Gather all the facts and opinions you need to establish whether what at first appeared to be the problem is in fact what must be tackled. Perhaps the apparent problem is really being caused by a more fundamental weakness which must be faced first.

Identify the real problem

For example: The budget is continuously being overrun. Is the problem due to our supervisors continually overspending on their budgets through poor planning? Or is it due to our asking the supervisors to work to an unrealistic budgeting system that is hindering rather than helping them to run their sections more efficiently?

You may also be faced with a series of related problems at times, and it may be difficult to sort out which are real and where to start.

For example: A valuable first export order is canceled (Problem 1) because the first shipment was three weeks late (Problem 2). It was late because it was sent to the wrong address (Problem 3) due to the shipping documentation being incorrectly completed (Problem 4). This was the result of administrative procedures and controls being far too loose (Problem 5), with no one anticipating that new procedures for export would be needed to avoid such shipping problems (Problem 6).

Six problems! But are they all real ones? Do they all require independent solution and action? And which comes first?

Since Problem 6 is the most fundamental, you may be tempted to start here. But there is a danger. Unless the focus is kept clearly on preventing similar situations from recurring, the temptation to indulge in a futile witch hunt may be overwhelming.

Problem 6 is real, and it requires specific attention. But so does Problem 1, and the canceled order is not only *serious* for the well-being of the organization, it is *urgent* too. So Problem 1 should be the top priority problem for attention.

Problems 2, 3, and 4 are not real problems. None of them should recur if Problem 5 is correctly solved. So the lack of adequate administrative procedures and controls is the next real problem to tackle.

Finally there's Problem 6. Although it is not *urgent*, the failure to anticipate that going into a new export venture might need administrative changes is probably the most *serious* problem of all. If my organization were moving into new fields without adequate planning, I would be feeling pretty edgy about it. I might wonder whether we planned to stay in business in the near future!

In summary then, the real problems that require specific independent attention are 1 (serious and urgent), 5 (urgent), and 6 (serious). Tackling them in this order seems to make the best sense.

When you have determined the real problem that deserves your top priority attention, you can then decide how to tackle it. Is it a problem that you have the authority to handle personally or should you refer it to higher levels? Is it a problem that is best handled by yourself, or is some type of discussion with your subordinates appropriate?

If discussion is needed, how important is the quality of the decision to be made and how important is the commitment of those who will be carrying it out? Bearing these points in mind, and also your skill as a discussion leader, which of the four approaches (Tell, Sell, Consult, or Participate) would be the best one for you to use?

Plan the discussion. Let's assume that you have decided to Participate (or at least to Consult) with your subordinates in handling the problem. Your next move is to plan the discussion. You will need to consider who should attend the discussion, the area to be covered in the discussion, and the specific objective you expect to reach during the time available.

Determining an objective is an important part of your planning because if you don't know where you are going, you are liable to end up far from your original goal. However, you only need to decide the general *type of action* you expect to come from the meeting, not specifically what you would do if required to act *without* calling a meeting.

For example: Your objective for discussing the reduction of hand accidents should be expressed as "Agree on how we will reduce hand accidents in the section" rather than "Agree to enforce use of gloves during all loading and unloading work." Obviously the second objective is going to turn a Participate discussion into a Consult or even a Sell discussion. This would greatly reduce the amount of involvement you would get from the group members in the discussion.

After defining the objective you will need to decide how to introduce the discussion and then develop a line of attack to follow during the problem solving.

Plan a line of attack

Without having some idea of the order in which to discuss each aspect of the problem, you probably won't make much progress toward your objective.

You could begin by establishing the causes of what is wrong; then you could evolve a number of ideas on how to eliminate or overcome these causes. Each of these ideas could be explored and evaluated, and in the final stage you could pick the best course of action.

Another line of attack might be to first decide on the ideal solution to the problem. As the next stage, you could discuss the difficulties inherent in this solution, and develop a compromise solution. Further decisions would then have to be made on how to implement that compromise and follow up the results.

There is no standard line of attack to follow, since every problem will suggest a different one. But if a discussion leader begins a discussion without any idea of how the discussion might be directed toward the objective, she is handing over complete responsibility for reaching the objective in the available time to the group members. In business, there are few effective discussion leaders who will go this far when allocating time to group discussion.

Arrange the meeting. Here you will need to ensure that those who will attend are suitably prepared for the meeting. They should know in advance what is to be discussed and what will be expected of them during the discussion. You should also ask for any information (statistics, sales records) that will be needed during the discussion. This will save considerable time during the meeting itself.

There will also be a few important physical arrangements to attend to. One of the most important is the seating arrangements. People need to be comfortable in their chairs, of course, or their attention will soon begin to wander. "The mind can absorb no more than the seat can endure" makes as much sense in a meeting as it ever did in the classroom.

Plan meeting arrangements carefully

But there is another key aspect to seating which is often overlooked. The way the chairs are arranged can actually influence the degree of participation you will achieve in your meeting.

Let's look at two typical arrangements: the long table with the leader at the head, and the square arrangement with the leader a part of the group.

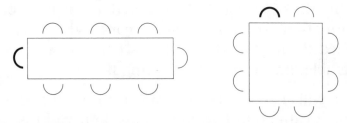

As you can see, the first arrangement makes much better use of the available table space and places the leader in a position of prominence most befitting her

exalted status. This arrangement would be appropriate in meetings where the purpose is to pass down
"The Word" from on high, with not too much backtalk
from the troops.

But what effect do you think this arrangement would
have on a problem-solving discussion where everyone needed to be in the act? Unless the leader worked
very hard to avoid it, the following pattern of discussion would develop.

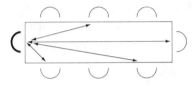

As you can see, all the discussion tends to be directed
to and from the leader. This is the role she is custom-
arily expected to play at the head of the table.

What would be far more effective would be a more
open exchange of information and ideas, like this.

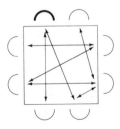

Research shows that the increased participation
depicted here is much easier to obtain with a "Round
Table" format than with a more conventional "Baron-
ial Hall" format. Maybe King Arthur had something!

Just one or two other meeting arrangements should
be mentioned. Don't forget that inconvenient timing,

continuous interruptions, lack of suitable handouts and visual aids (flipchart, overhead projector), inadequate ventilation, or liquid refreshments can all have a disastrous effect on the success of your meeting. So don't overlook these points either.

Summary

Identify the real problem.
>Obtain the necessary facts and opinions.
>Determine the top priority problem.
>Decide the extent and type of discussion needed.

Plan the discussion.
>Consider who should attend.
>Decide the area to be covered.
>Set an objective for the discussion.
>Decide upon a possible line of attack.

Arrange the meeting.
>Make sure everyone is prepared.
>Take care of all physical arrangements.

Cliff Aitken paused in the middle of his morning shave. He looked at his reflection in the mirror and sighed.

"Those damned Aristocrat glasses are really beginning to get me down," he thought. "No, not the glasses; they're magnificent, graceful. It's finding the solution to the breakage problem. That's what's getting me down."

He continued his shave. "Why haven't we solved the problem in nearly a year of investigation and discussion?"

He paused again. "Have we identified the real problem?" he wondered.

Suddenly Cliff realized the problem wasn't the breakages, or even the packaging. The problem was the careless handling of the boxes.

"Solve that problem and there would be no breakages," he thought. "But there are so many different people that handle those boxes on that long journey from factory to home. . . ."

Cliff sighed again and returned to his shaving.

Later, in his office, Cliff drafted an agenda for next Monday's meeting. The subject? What he now called "The Careless Handling Problem."

1. Redefine the problem.

2. Establish the most probable causes.

3. Generate alternative solutions.

4. Evaluate alternatives.

41

5. Select a solution.

6. Plan implementation.

"That should do it," Cliff thought. "It's logical, it's systematic, and it should help everyone to make progress."

"Send this agenda to everyone who will be attending the Monday meeting," he told his secretary. "And look after the usual arrangements, please. Particularly incoming calls. I don't want any interruptions. We've *got* to come up with a solution this time."

Now let's see what you think . . .

a) How well did Cliff prepare for this critical meeting?

b) Has he at long last identified the real problem correctly?

c) What about his planning for the discussion? Would you have done anything differently?

d) And the meeting arrangements? Was anything else needed?

You guessed it. We'll be back to **Broken Glass** in just a moment. But first let's consider the opening stage of the discussion itself . . .

Step 2: Introduce the Discussion

Clarify the objective. Your first task during the meeting is to make sure everyone understands what is to be discussed and why. All the relevant facts and opinions needed to understand the problem should be established. Many of these you will provide yourself, but don't overlook those in the group who can draw on their experience to confirm or add to what you have said.

Clarify the objective

For example: "So that's what happened as soon as we tried to start up yesterday evening. It looks to me as though there's something wrong with our maintenance schedule, but of course, this may not be the trouble. Can anyone remember something like this happening before?"

The specific objective of the discussion should then be stated. This is where you make sure that the group members know exactly what is expected of them during the meeting. This is also where you draw the limits of the discussion, deciding what will not be discussed as well as what will.

For example: "We are all very much concerned with this problem and I will appreciate your assistance in working out a solution that each of you can apply in your own section. We don't have time to work out every detail during this meeting, but we must agree on the broad approach we will all be following."

Stimulate group interest. Now you will need to show each member how reaching the objective will help him. How is the objective important to him personally; to his section; to the company? Providing answers to these questions will establish the basis for a friendly team spirit throughout the discussion.

You will also want to let your group know that there is no need for the excessive formality of a large meeting. In group discussion you can live without "Mr. Chairman, Sir, may I, through you, move that the Honorary Secretary open one or two windows in here?"

A useful way of creating the right atmosphere is to wind up the introductions by suggesting a line of attack that might be followed during the discussion, and then getting group understanding and agreement on this point before beginning discussion on the problem.

For example: "Now, before we begin, let's agree on how we should discuss this problem. Suppose we begin by discussing the expected effects on profitability in each of our operations. This should help us to decide on priorities for action. Then we can decide what should be done in each area in turn, and agree on deadlines. Does that seem like a logical order to follow in our discussion?"

If you get full commitment to both the objective and to the best way to progress to this objective, your job in controlling the discussion that follows will be very much easier.

Summary

Clarify the objective.
    Explain the problem to be discussed.
    Establish the relevant facts and opinions.
    State the specific objective of discussion.

Stimulate group interest.
    Clarify the importance of the objective.
    Encourage a friendly team spirit.
    Get agreement on the line of attack for the
        problem.

Cliff Aitken shuffled his papers to bring his meeting agenda to the surface. Then he looked up.

"We're all here, so let's start."

He looked around the table. "Well, did you all receive the agenda I sent you?" There was a murmur of assent.

"Do you agree that this is a logical way to discuss the problem?"

Again, general murmurs of agreement.

"I'm not sure I understand what you mean by 'Redefine the Problem,'" said Bill warily.

"Well, Bill, it occurred to me that the mistake we've been making is defining the problem as stem breakages. All your efforts as a result have been aimed at preventing those breakages."

"True," nodded Bill.

"Well, you established months ago that the cause of the breakages was careless handling, not design or manufacturing faults."

"Right again," agreed Bill.

"If that's so, shouldn't we now be spending our time concentrating on finding the causes of the careless handling and deciding how to reduce them?"

"I'm not sure I see the difference," said Bill, now looking really puzzled.

"Can anyone help clear up this point?" asked Cliff, looking around the group.

"What you're saying, Mr. Aitken," offered Cas, "is that we've been concentrating too heavily on how to avoid breakages when the boxes are carelessly handled. What we should be doing is trying to prevent the careless handling."

"But we did try that," cut in Bill. "Don't you remember? We reworked the discount structure to make it more attractive for the stores to prevent breakages."

"And what happened?" asked Cliff.

"Returns came down by nearly 4 percent," replied Bill.

"Yes, and that was the only worthwhile improvement we've seen in ten months of fooling around," said Frank scathingly.

"Back off, Frank," said Cliff. "It was Bill's idea and it worked. Let's not forget that. He must have been on the right track at the time, but we didn't follow through. Why don't we all try building on Bill's idea of reducing the careless handling? I'm sure that's the key to success. What do you say?"

Cliff looked at each person in turn. One by one, they nodded in agreement. "Why not?" "Sure." "Suits me." "What have we got to lose?" "OK."

Cliff picked up his agenda.

"So let's take a shot at our first item on the agenda — Redefining the Problem. Let's see if we can get something up on the flipchart."

Let's have your opinion now . . .

a) How well has Cliff succeeded in getting his team off to a good start?

b) How clear is the objective to each member of the group? What would you have done differently?

c) Is the group really interested in contributing fully to the discussion? In solving the problem? How could Cliff have stimulated group interest more effectively?

Another episode of **Broken Glass** will follow shortly, after we talk about how to lead a problem-solving discussion . . .

Guide the group. Once your group knows where it is going and has agreed on the best way to get there, you can throw the discussion open. But you will still need to guide that discussion.

Get them started by asking a few questions which will stimulate discussion on the first stage. It is often useful to go to the individuals who have had special experience in the field. They will help you to get the discussion moving.

Don't dominate the discussion

Make sure, however, that no one, *not even yourself as the discussion leader*, is allowed to dominate the discussion. There is no surer way of killing the interest of the rest of the group. One of your major functions is to ensure that the discussion is shared fairly among all who wish to make a contribution.

This calls for skillfully observing all the group members. It means stimulating the quieter members and controlling the more talkative ones. It also involves supporting the right of everyone to have his opinion considered, no matter how controversial it may seem.

Let's pause here to ask a question: As a discussion leader, how do you feel when all the members of your group are nodding their heads at you like those stuffed animals you see in the rear windows of cars? Hypnotic, isn't it? You can get a real glow from that sort of thing but—watch out!

"The first rule in decision making," says Peter Drucker, "is that one does not make a decision unless there is disagreement." This may sound surprising, but the thinking behind it is really quite simple. A solution to a problem to which there is apparently no alternative is a very dangerous solution. There is *always* more than one way to solve a problem, and if we can't see the alternatives, we probably don't understand the problem fully.

Therefore the effective discussion leader looks for, rather than discourages, disagreement. She knows that by exploring the *reasons* people think differently, she will improve everyone's understanding of the problem. She avoids starting out with the thought that one proposed course of action is right and all others must be wrong. She also guards against thinking "I am right and he is wrong." Instead she continually asks herself, "Now why is *he* seeing it differently from the rest of us? What have *we* missed?" And then she keeps asking questions out loud until her silent questions have been answered. This is the way to make decisions which are based on *all* the available evidence, not just on special preferences or pet theories.

Of course, not all types of disagreement are helpful in a discussion. Members bring their own personal interests and prejudices to every meeting. Sometimes these can hinder discussion rather than help you toward your objective. When members begin to help themselves to your discussion time, you should know how to bring them back to helping the team. Some of the situations you could meet are depicted in the drawing at the back of this book (page 93), together with suggestions on what to do in each case.

Keep the discussion moving forward. Group discussion meetings can be very time consuming unless properly handled by the discussion leader. Much time

Keep the discussion moving forward

can be wasted through misunderstandings of the points being made. Whenever you suspect this might be happening, you should rephrase what has been said and check this with the person concerned. For example: "Let's be sure we all understand your point, Peggy. Are you suggesting that we've been discussing the wrong problem?" It is pointless to continue discussing a contribution until everyone is clear on what has been said.

Time can also be wasted through members sidetracking the discussion, grinding their favorite axes, or allowing personal conflicts in the group to color their thinking. This is the time to gently remind them of the objective set for the discussion and of the line of attack agreed upon.

And what about side discussions? How *should* you handle the two cozy guys at the far end of the table who keep making private remarks to one another? It looks like they're really enjoying themselves. And you're not sure how relevant their witticisms are to the subject being discussed.

You could leave them alone, of course, but sooner or later they'll distract others in the group. In the circumstances, you may be tempted to demonstrate your truly sparkling wit. "Everyone likes a good laugh," you'd like to say. "Won't you two clowns share your joke with the rest of us?" Or even sharper, "What are you two turkeys at the back gobbling about?"

That sort of thing is sure to raise a smile from the rest of the group, but what kind of reaction can you expect from the two unfortunates you've just turned your spotlight on? Probably protest, justification, resentment, and withdrawal—at the very least!

So let's try something a little more subtle. "Bob, Jim. You seem to have spotted one or two things we've missed. Won't you help by sharing your insights with the rest of us?"

Another way of discouraging sidetracking and encouraging the group members to keep pulling together is to regularly sum up the progress made. This can be done whenever the group appears doubtful on the direction to take. It should *always* be done at the conclusion of each agenda item and used to introduce discussion on the next stage.

For example: "Well, we seem to have covered what actually happened pretty thoroughly. Now before we go on to discuss the differences that existed yesterday, compared to the hundred times this job has gone without a hitch, is there anything else we have overlooked?"

Occasionally the line of attack agreed upon at the outset will seem less helpful as the discussion progresses. If an alternative is suggested which the group agrees will speed up progress toward the objective, do not hesitate to adopt it. It is the objective that is important, not the way you get to it.

And so with your objective ever present in mind, you will thread your way through a maze of blind alleys and diversions toward the point where decisions can be made.

Summary

Guide the group.
> Stimulate discussion on the first stage.
> Draw on the special experience of individuals.
> Ensure that discussion is shared fairly among all members.

Explore the reasons for disagreement between members.

Keep the discussion moving forward.

Ensure that all contributions are understood.

Keep the discussion on track.

Sum up progress made regularly.

Lead the group through the remaining stages toward the objective.

"Let's take stock of how far we've come," said Cliff Aitken.

He looked at the flipchart. "We've redefined our problem as 'Shipping, wholesale, and retail employees are handling Aristocrat boxes in a way that causes an unacceptable number of breakages, even where box strength and padding have been improved beyond normal company standards.'"

He turned over the sheet. "We've also agreed on a number of possible causes. Let's read through them."

Work pressure	Poor discipline
Lack of interest	Insufficient incentive
Carelessness	Quality of employees
Poor attitude	Impatience
Irresponsibility	Ignoring of warning labels

"Anything else you'd like to add?"

Cliff glanced around the group, paused, and then went on. "It seems to me that there are a few of these that are way out of our control."

He turned to the flipchart and crossed out *Work pressure* and *Quality of employees*. "We couldn't do much about these, could we?"

"Agreed," said Ted loudly.

"So let's focus on the remainder," Cliff continued. "How could we classify these in some way to make them easier to handle?"

"It seems to me," said Cas, "that the remainder break down into two groups. 'Poor discipline' and 'Insufficient incentive' both relate to the way the employees concerned are supervised. All the rest amount to the Don't Care attitude you find in this type of person nowadays. In my day things were different. I remember when I started my first job . . . ."

"That's a valuable contribution you've just made, Cas," cut in Cliff. "What you're saying is that any solutions we consider should be aimed either at improving supervision or directly at improving employee attitudes."

"I'm not sure there's much more we could do about the supervision," Bill responded. "After all, the discount structure now makes it really attractive to prevent breakages. I think we should talk about how we might improve employee attitudes."

"I can't wait to hear how you're going to do that," sneered Frank.

"How *we* are going to do that, Frank," corrected Cliff. "But you don't feel it can be done?"

"No, I don't."

"Frank, as Distribution Manager, you are probably closer to these people than any of us. Won't you tell us why you think changing their attitudes isn't practical?"

"They handle everything from virtually indestructible nuts and bolts to our super-brittle glassware. It's all packaged in similar cardboard cartons and both extremes are often batched together for shipping to the same retail store. It's heavy, tiring work and they often have to meet very tight deadlines. It's just too much to expect them to develop a delicate touch when they come across a batch of our boxes. That's why I think it isn't practical."

"You may have a point there, Frank," conceded Cliff.

"But they can't think they're handling nuts and bolts when they're packing our boxes," Bill cut in. "There's the weight for one thing, and there's the orange and black warning label for another."

Frank brought his fist down on the table, hard.

"If the labels were etched in neon lights, those people wouldn't pay any attention to them. They're just not interested in what's in the boxes. Only where they're going and how many."

There was a long silence. Cliff looked around the table.

"Jean," he said. "You're looking very thoughtful. Do you have something to contribute?"

"I was wondering, Mr. Aitken, whether they would handle our boxes like nuts and bolts if they knew there were delicate wine glasses inside." She turned to Frank. "What do you think, Frank?"

"You mean as compared with tough, commercial water tumblers?" Cliff broke in.

"Yes, that's right, Mr. Aitken. Frank?"

"I don't think it would make any difference," said Frank sourly.

"Let's check that around, Frank," said Cliff. "Ted, what's your opinion?"

"I think Jean's got something there. Suppose we were to replace that warning label with a full-color print of an Aristocrat glass, the one we use for counter displays. Wouldn't that get the warning message across better?"

There were murmurs of agreement around the table. Even Frank began to look thoughtful.

"Now we're humming," beamed Cliff. "Can anyone build on Ted's suggestion?"

"I don't know whether this is practical," said Jean hesitantly, "but what if you could actually see the glasses themselves? You know, through the top of the box."

"You mean a transparent plastic lid?" asked Bill quickly.

"Yes, something like that."

Cliff turned to Cas. "Do you think that could be done, Cas?"

"Sure. It would mean designing a completely new box, with maybe a recessed lid. But it could be done."

"If we had a really attractive box with a transparent lid, we could use the box itself for counter displays," added Ted enthusiastically.

"And how do you think your smart boxes will look after they've been handled a dozen times in transit?" asked Frank.

"Hold it, Frank," said Bill. "We could pack four boxes together back-to-back and then cover them with transparent shrink film. That would protect the boxes and yet still show the glasses inside. A kind of double protection."

"Great idea, Bill," said Ted, looking pointedly at Frank. But Frank had turned away and was gazing absently out the window.

Now for your thoughts . . .

a) How well do you think Cliff led this problem-solving discussion?

b) How effectively did he guide the group through the discussion? What would you have done differently?

c) What about the way he kept the discussion moving forward? Did he make the best use of the time? Do you feel any aspect could have been handled better?

d) Which method (Tell, Sell, Consult, or Participate) did Cliff use? Was it appropriate? Why?

Yes, we have one final episode of **Broken Glass** for you to analyze. You'll find it at the end of the next section on concluding the discussion . . .

Step 4: Conclude the Discussion

Sum up overall progress. As soon as you feel that you are ready to come to a final decision, you should summarize the progress made. But don't assume that everyone agrees that all the relevant aspects of the problem have been considered. Ask them if there is anything important that has been overlooked, and discuss this further until everyone is satisfied.

Don't cut off discussion until everyone is satisfied

Clarify action to be taken. There are always many things that must be decided before you can conclude a group discussion, but "*What* is to be done?" is the question that must be answered first.

If someone suggests "nothing," don't be too quick to discount her. Occasionally the wisest solution to a problem is to do just that: nothing. And then watch closely and cross your fingers, of course.

Normally you will lead the group to an agreed decision on what is to be done, in what order. There are times, however, when although you can get the group to agree that *something* has to be done, this is about *all* you are able to get agreement on. Exactly *what* has to be done looks as though it might take another week or two to decide. This is when you will have to weigh all the evidence for yourself and decide *for* the group what has to be done.

If agreement cannot be reached, make a decision

If you are wise you will tell them of your decision with all your remaining patience and tact. No one likes to have his ideas overruled, but he feels much better about it if he has at least had his say and knows that his suggestions have been considered.

For example: "Well, I can see that our time is running out and we will just have to cut our discussion short.

It seems we are about equally divided on whether or not to call in a consultant to help us with this problem. There are clearly excellent arguments for both sides. However, remembering the urgency of correcting the present situation,I feel we do need some expert help from outside. Now, let's discuss how we might get this assistance without some of the real dangers that have been pointed out."

Yes, "*How* is it to be done?" is usually the question that follows immediately after "*What* is to be done?" Most of your concluding discussion will be taken up with these two questions.

Three more questions must also be settled before you're through. "*Who* is to do it?" usually comes next, followed by "*Where*" and then "*When* is it to be done?" In discussing *when* don't forget to set target finishing dates as well as target starting dates, and to agree on how progress is to be reported.

When you have decided on each of these points and made sure everyone understands the action to be taken, you can at last close the discussion.

Summary

Sum up overall progress.

Ensure that all relevant aspects have been considered.

Clarify action to be taken.

Bring the group to a decision on a specific course of action.

Ensure that everyone understands the action to be taken.

"It seems to me," said Cliff, looking at his watch, "that we've had a real breakthrough here this afternoon. We've clarified the problem that has been bugging us for so many months. We've put our finger on two main causes: poor supervision and poor attitude. We've already done something about the first and, in discussing the second, it seems we've spotted a third cause, poor communication of our warning message. We've come up with a number of possible solutions to this problem, some of which have promising promotional spin-offs.   Are we ready now to decide exactly what we will do and how we will do it?"

Cliff looked at each person in turn and held his gaze until he expressed his agreement. He was surprised when Frank also nodded without further discussion.

"Bill," said Cliff, "will you sum up what needs to be done, as you see it?"

"Well, first we need to design a combined shipping and display box with a transparent lid."

"Right," said Cliff, "and who will do that? Will you and Cas work together on that, Bill?"

Ted looked as though he wanted to say something, but before he could speak, Cliff went on.

"What's next, Bill?"

"I'd certainly like to look into the shrink film idea to protect the boxes."

"Fine," said Cliff. "Anything else?"

"No, I don't think so."

"Bill, there is one more thing. As soon as you've got everything worked out, I'd like you to get together with Jean to go over the cost implications. OK, Jean?"

"Certainly, Mr. Aitken."

"Well, that just about wraps it up." Cliff smiled warmly at each member of his team. "Thank you all very much."

Here's your last chance . . .

a) How effective was Cliff in concluding this discussion?

b) What did you think of his summary of overall progress?

c) What about the way he clarified the action to be taken? Was there room for improvement here?

d) How would you rate the quality of the decisions that were made and their chances of success?

e) How would you rate the commitment that these decisions will have from all those who are concerned with their implementation?

When you have answered all these questions, compare your ideas with the model answers which begin on page 73.

Final Summary of Discussion-Leading Skills

Step 1: Prepare for the Discussion

Identify the real problem.

Obtain the necessary facts and opinions.

Determine your top priority problem.

Decide the extent and type of discussion needed.

Plan the discussion.

Consider who should attend.

Decide the area to be covered.

Set an objective for the discussion.

Decide upon a possible line of attack.

Arrange the meeting.

Make sure everyone is prepared.

Take care of all physical arrangements.

Step 2: Introduce the Discussion

Clarify the objective.

Explain the problem to be discussed.

Establish the relevant facts and opinions.

State the specific objective of discussion.

Stimulate group interest.

Clarify the importance of the objective.

Encourage a friendly team spirit.

Get agreement on the line of attack for the problem.

Step 3: Lead the Discussion

Guide the group.

Stimulate discussion on the first stage.

Draw on the special experience of individuals.

Ensure that discussion is shared fairly among all members.

Explore the reasons for disagreement between members.

Keep the discussion moving forward.

Ensure that all contributions are understood.

Keep the discussion on track.

Sum up progress made regularly.

Lead the group through the remaining stages toward the objective.

Step 4: Conclude the Discussion

Sum up overall progress.

Ensure that all relevant aspects have been considered.

Clarify action to be taken.

Bring the group to a decision on a specific course of action.

Ensure that everyone understands the action to be taken.

Last Word

If you do a good job of discussion leading, you will arrive at a sound decision which also has the commitment of those concerned with carrying it out. When this happens, the results of your decisions may still bring you disappointments, but you can be sure that they will be fewer and less shattering than in the past. In the field of human affairs, can we expect more?

Model Answers to the *Broken Glass* Exercises

Part 1

a) Cliff clearly has confidence in Bill and has given him full responsibility to investigate the problem. He is quite right to resist the easy solution of thickening the stems. If there were an inherent weakness in the thin stems, breakages in the home would not be rare.

b) Cliff is using the Consult method because although Bill has a free hand in the investigation, he is reporting progress regularly to Cliff. It is also clear that Cliff has retained responsibility for deciding on the action to be taken.

c) Cliff's approach is basically sound because he is leaving all the details to Bill. He has reserved only the key decisions for himself. However, it seems as though Bill could use a little more support. He doesn't sound too sure of himself and would probably welcome more participation from Cliff. For example, Bill needs more detailed reaction to his ideas on thickening the stems (why they shouldn't) and on revising the discount structure (why they should).

Part 2

a) Not at all effectively. Apart from his opening remarks, which sound pretty threatening, he has virtually taken no part. As a result he has a fight on his hands between Bill and Frank.

b) No, it isn't clear. The group members know that Cliff is dissatisfied with their progress, but that's all. What is the meeting expected to accomplish? To obtain more information or ideas, to coordinate action, to recommend action, or decide action? It could be any of these and, unless they know what is expected of them, it will be very difficult for them to function effectively as a team.

c) Cliff just hasn't played his role as a discussion leader. He has let Bill initiate the discussion with an attempted justification and then merely smiled when Frank attacked Bill for lack of progress. He should have led them into the discussion on a much more positive note and quickly stepped in to check the exchange between Bill and Frank.

d) The friendly team spirit is also conspicuous by its absence. The game to play seems to be "pass the hot potato," according to Frank and Bill. Unless Cliff quickly takes control of the discussion, the chances of achieving anything constructive in this meeting are close to zero.

Part 3

a) Cliff is really beginning to get himself together. He has recovered well after the disastrous start we saw in Part 2.

b) He has certainly stimulated Bill, Jean, and Ted to take part. However, he did this by directing the questions at each person individually. He has done nothing to stimulate others in the group to participate in the discussion. For example, he could have encouraged group members to ask questions at the end of Bill's progress report. Cliff is still apparently using the Consult method, but this time in a group meeting.

c) Cliff seems to have overreacted to his lack of control at the start of this meeting. Now almost no one is speaking unless spoken to. For example, Cas had to cut in to get a word in edgewise. Because of this, the time spent is very short but, if the objective is to generate possible solutions, more time would certainly be justified.

d) Cliff comes out pretty well in the support department. He backed up both Bill and Cas when they were attacked. But what about Ted? Didn't he deserve a bit of support too? For example, Cliff might have softened his reprimand by saying "Ted, you're quite right to be worried about remaining competitive, as I'm sure Cas is also, but he may have a point about the price."

e) Cliff seems aware of the more obvious conflicts (Bill vs. Frank and Cas vs. Ted), but how good is he at spotting his own tendency to favoritism (Bill and Cas)? And what about Cliff's resistance to fuller participation? He certainly doesn't sound as though he has much confidence in his team's ability to solve this problem. Is he aware of the handicap this attitude is placing on his team? His final remarks about "really needing your ideas" suggest he is beginning to realize this.

Part 4

a) Better than any of his previous meetings, apparently. He seems to be aware now that more careful planning is needed if real progress is to be accomplished. However, he missed a few things, as we shall see.

b) He has begun to challenge his previous assumptions about the problem they have been facing, and this can only help the problem-solving process. At the moment his definition of the problem is much more specific and focuses on a deficiency, the cause of which is *not* known. However, his definition is not as clear as it might be. The fact that he has placed this as the first item on the agenda suggests he realizes that more work is needed.

He also seems to have accepted that a much more participative group discussion is needed if a solution, one better than any he could generate alone or with any one individual, is to be found.

c) His planning is adequate at best. He does not appear to have assessed whether the five members of his executive team are the best people to attend this meeting. Considering that the problem has been defined as careless handling by employees outside Aitken Glass, surely one or two people from their shippers, wholesalers, and retailers should have been included.

The objective of the meeting also seems to have been overlooked. When his executives receive the agenda, they will know what is to be discussed and how it could be tackled. However, they will still not know what part they are expected to play in the discussion and hence will not be able to prepare for the meeting adequately.

d) Cliff's arrangements for the meeting also seem sketchy. Shouldn't he have provided those attending with more than the subject, the objective (as already discussed), and the agenda? For example, what happened to Ted's report on the implications of a price hike to cover the cost of the breakages?

Part 5

a) On the surface, Cliff has succeeded fairly well. He has clarified the problem to some extent, and has obtained their agreement (if not their commitment) to focus on the problem as restated.

b) The objective, stated in terms of what will be expected of them in the discussion, was very vague ("Why don't we all try building on Bill's idea of reducing the careless handling?"). The group members don't know what kind of result should come from the meeting: a recommendation, decision, plan, or what?

c) Judging by the half-hearted enthusiasm they displayed at the end of the episode, their interest in this meeting is lukewarm at best. Clarifying the specific objective would surely have helped, but more was needed. If they found a solution, what was in it for them? Frank and Bill would certainly be better off, but what about the others? When you think about it, all of them stood to gain something personally and also as a member of the Aitken management team. Cliff had a chance to really sell them on finding a solution, but he let it pass right by.

On top of this, his attempt at generating real team spirit was weak and he really didn't get commitment to the line of attack he had outlined in his agenda. Better preparation for the meeting would have corrected most of these weaknesses.

Part 6

a) Apart from a few lapses, Cliff handled this part of his meeting better than the earlier sessions. He filled the four roles of a discussion leader (stimulate, control, support, observe) in a well-balanced way. Toward the end he had built up their interest to the point where they had begun to combine forces to cope with Frank's objections.

b) Cliff stimulated discussion on each stage very well, although he didn't make obvious use of his agenda. Since they hadn't worked out the agenda together, letting the discussion flow naturally was a wise move. He also drew on the special experience of individuals, particularly that of Frank and Cas. Cliff brought everyone into the discussion at some time, and he explored Frank's disagreement very effectively.

c) Cliff kept the discussion moving forward well. He helped to clarify vague contributions and avoided wasting time on Cas' reminiscences. He also summed up well at the end of the first two stages ("Redefining the problem" and "Establishing the most probable causes").

d) Cliff clearly used the Participate method in the latter part of this meeting. And it was this change from his customary Consult method that produced the success of his meeting. Compare, for example, the degree of enthusiasm and problem-solving effort at the beginning with the level achieved towards the end.

Part 7

a) Cliff drew the threads together fairly well at the end. However, apparently distracted by a new solution and by the time this unfamiliar group participation was taking, Cliff skipped over the latter stages of his agenda very rapidly. None of the suggested solutions was properly evaluated during the meeting and any snags that might have been considered will now only emerge later.

b) Cliff's summary was helpful, adding a new dimension to Cas' classification of the main causes. He also checked that they were ready before taking them into the last few stages of the discussion.

c) It was a good idea to get Bill, who would be directly responsible for implementing their decisions, to clarify the action to be taken. However, Cliff allowed himself to slip back into an earlier role when he asked Bill who would design the new box and then answered his own question. Had he not done so, there is no doubt that Ted would have been invited to join the design team as well.

Cliff apparently forgot to clarify several future concerns. He did not set a target date for the design committee to report on the new box and its cost implications. He also did not have the group discuss and agree on how progress should be reported.

d) The decisions made were very promising and, if the problem has been correctly identified and the solutions are practical, should bring about a significant reduction in breakages. They would have to be carefully followed up to ensure that some other factor had not been overlooked. The transparent box solution should really be tested in a pilot study before committing to a full-scale changeover.

e) Apart from Frank, who seems to be a very hard nut to crack, the commitment of Cliff's team to their solution appears high. A little more open discussion at the end of the meeting, when Cliff seemed in too much of a hurry to finish, would have confirmed this.

However, the commitment of the management of Aitken Glass' shippers, wholesalers, and retailers hasn't been considered. Again, the pilot study trial could be used to attain this commitment. Certainly their support in finally solving the **Broken Glass** case should not be taken for granted.

Self-Test

If you would like to further check your understanding of the points made in this book, try this test.

For each of the questions, both correct and incorrect answers are given. Quite often more than one answer is correct and more than one is incorrect, so don't be content to choose only one answer to each question.

Place a ✓ opposite each answer you consider correct and an ✗ opposite each answer you consider incorrect. You will find the answer key on page 89. If you want to find out where you went wrong, turn to the page reference indicated in parentheses below each question.

1. The results you get from the solutions to problems you handle usually depend on
   a. the quality of your decisions. _____
   b. the commitment to your decisions. _____
   c. neither of these. _____

   (See pages 3-4.)

2. In all problems, the quality of the decisions you make is
   a. less important _____
   b. more important _____
   c. sometimes more, sometimes less important _____

than the commitment of those who carry out the decision.

(See pages 3-4.)

3. Running a group discussion to help solve a problem will usually

  a. reduce decision quality. _____

  b. increase commitment to the decision. _____

  c. increase quality and commitment. _____

    (See pages 4-6.)

4. Allowing individuals to participate in making decisions that concern them also develops their

  a. truthfulness. _____

  b. responsibility. _____

  c. intelligence. _____

  d. initiative. _____

  e. team spirit. _____

    (See page 6.)

5. There are four main approaches in handling a problem through group discussion. They are

  a. Sell. _____

  b. Suggest. _____

  c. Offer. _____

  d. Consult. _____

  e. Determine. _____

  f. Tell. _____

  g. Participate. _____

    (See pages 6-7.)

6. If we arranged four of these approaches in order of increasing effectiveness in obtaining commitment to the decision (starting with the least effective), the order would be

a. Sell, Tell, Consult, Participate. _____

b. Tell, Sell, Consult, Participate. _____

c. Tell, Sell, Participate, Consult. _____

(See pages 6-7.)

7. You should tell the group members what is expected of them in handling the problem

a. before the discussion. _____

b. when opening the discussion. _____

c. only if you are asked. _____

d. only if they go off the track. _____

(See pages 8-9, 37, and 44.)

8. The main things which you can recognize in an effective group discussion are

a. a clear aim. _____

b. a lack of disagreement. _____

c. a group leader. _____

d. a frank and open atmosphere. _____

(See pages 15-17.)

9. If you feel that one member's contributions are not much use to the discussion, you should

a. tell him so. _____

b. explore his contributions. _____

c. overlook them. _____

d. guide him gently back to the main topic. _____

(See pages 15-17 and 24-25.)

10. During the discussion, you must continually

a. observe   _____

b. control   _____

c. stimulate   _____

d. agree with   _____

e. persuade   _____

f. support   _____

the group members.

(See pages 21-27.)

11. When faced with a problem which concerns your people, you should always

a. get the necessary facts.   _____

b. identify the real problem.   _____

c. plan the discussion.   _____

(See pages 33-37.)

12. Suppose you have decided to Participate with your subordinates in solving the problem of inducting new workers. Which way would you state the objective of the discussion?

a. Decide the contents of a three-day program for new workers coming into the section.   _____

b. Decide whether new workers in the section should be taken around by the personnel officer or by one of our supervisors.   _____

   c. Decide how to improve the way we intro-
      duce new workers into the section. _____

   (See pages 35-36.)

13. Discussions seldom progress the way you expect.
Thus, once you have decided your objective, the
next thing to do is

   a. brief those who will attend. _____

   b. think of a discussion sequence you
      could follow. _____

   (See pages 36-37.)

14. In preparing for a group discussion, you should
always arrange for

   a. adequate ventilation. _____

   b. a telephone in the room. _____

   c. comfortable seats. _____

   d. seats placed in rows. _____

   e. one free hour. _____

    f. water/tea/coffee to be available. _____

   g. a secretary to take minutes. _____

   h. a film to capture their interest. _____

   (See pages 37-40.)

15. You should stimulate interest in achieving the
objective of the discussion

   a. at the outset. _____

   b. during the discussion. _____

   c. at the conclusion. _____

d. when any person clearly indicates he is
   not concerned. _____

(See pages 21 and 44-45.)

16. You should call on individuals who have had
    special experience in the area being discussed

   a. to help get the discussion moving. _____

   b. to help establish the facts. _____

   c. to provide all the answers. _____

   d. to ensure that the biggest contributors
      are those with the most experience. _____

   (See pages 43 and 51.)

17. Time will be wasted during the discussion by

   a. misunderstandings. _____

   b. sidetracking. _____

   c. summaries of progress. _____

   d. rephrasing of ideas. _____

   e. axe grinding. _____

   f. personal conflicts. _____

   g. changing the line of attack. _____

   (See pages 53-55.)

18. Once you have summed up the overall progress
    made and clarified *what* has to be done, *how* and
    where it has to be done, and also *who* is to do it,
    you can safely

   a. close the discussion. _____

   b. discuss the final point. _____

   (See pages 63-65.)

19. If you have just run a group discussion throughout which everyone was in agreement on the problem and its solution, you should

   a. give yourself a star. _____

   b. wonder why there was no disagreement. _____

   c. sigh with relief. _____

   d. wonder if you discussed the real problem. _____

   e. wonder if there was a problem to discuss. _____

   (See pages 52-53.)

20. Now that you know more about group discussion leading, you will be able to

   a. lead meetings which should be more effective. _____

   b. run better meetings from now on. _____

   c. develop your discussion leading skills more quickly. _____

   (See page ix.)

Answers to Self-Test

Circle each error you made in your test.

1. a. ✔	2. a. ✘	3. a. ✘	4. a. ✘	5. a. ✔
b. ✔	b. ✘	b. ✔	b. ✔	b. ✘
c. ✘	c. ✔	c. ✔	c. ✘	c. ✘
			d. ✔	d. ✔
			e. ✔	e. ✘
				f. ✔
				g. ✔

6. a. ✘	7. a. ✔	8. a. ✔	9. a. ✘	10. a. ✔
b. ✔	b. ✔	b. ✘	b. ✔	b. ✔
c. ✘	c. ✘	c. ✔	c. ✘	c. ✔
	d. ✘	d. ✔	d. ✔	d. ✘
				e. ✘
				f. ✔

11. a. ✔	12. a. ✘	13. a. ✘	14. a. ✔	15. a. ✔
b. ✔	b. ✘	b. ✔	b. ✘	b. ✔
c. ✘	c. ✔		c. ✔	c. ✔
			d. ✘	d. ✘
			e. ✘	
			f. ✔	
			g. ✘	
			h. ✘	

16. a. ✔   17. a. ✔   18. a. ✘   19. a. ✘   20. a. ✔
    b. ✔   b. ✔   b. ✔   b. ✔   b. ✘
    c. ✘   c. ✘   c. ✘   c. ✔
    d. ✘   d. ✘   d. ✔
                  e. ✔   e. ✔
                  f. ✔
                  g. ✘

How Well Did You Do?

Six errors or less — give yourself ★★★★★

Seven to twenty errors — better look up a few of those reference pages given in parentheses

More than twenty errors — better go back to page 1 and reread this book

What to Do when a Group Member . . .

1. **Wants a fight:** Don't get involved. Explore his ideas and let the group decide their value.
2. **Would like to help:** Encourage him frequently to give his ideas, particularly when discussion is bogging down.
3. **Begins to split hairs:** Acknowledge his point but remind him of the objective and the time limit.
4. **Just keeps talking:** Interrupt tactfully. Ask him a question to bring him back to the point being discussed.
5. **Seems afraid to speak:** Ask him easy questions. Give him credit when possible and make him feel important.
6. **Grinds his own axe:** Recognize his self-interests and ask him if he can see an answer to his own objections.
7. **Is just not interested:** Ask him about his work and how the discussion could help him. If it can't, excuse him from the discussion.
8. **Acts superior:** Recognize his ability and ask him the most challenging questions.
9. **Wants to show how clever he is:** Watch out for his trick questions. Pass them back to the group to answer.

Michael Renton is an international management consultant specializing in the training and development field. He operates out of Johannesburg, South Africa, where he is a partner in a firm offering a multiplicity of services in the human sciences.

Mr. Renton has a University Honours Degree in Social and Industrial Psychology, which was awarded Cum Laude in 1962. He has over 15 years' practical experience in personnel work and has worked as a consultant since 1966.

One of Mr. Renton's many outside activities is car racing. He has a national hill climbing record which he achieved with a home-built racing car; he is also the winner of a six-hour endurance race for production cars.